# 37

## BIBLICAL HANDS-ON LESSONS TO
## ACTIVATE THE DREAMER & SEER

*See. Hear. Respond. Activate your child's God-given gifts.*

# MONTIA JANUARY

ISBN: 979-8-9948680-0-3 (for book)
ISBN: 979-8-9948680-1-0 (for ebook)
ISBN: 979-8-9948680-2-7 (for journal)

Published by: Montia January First Edition

Printed in the United States of America

# TABLE OF CONTENTS

# FORWARD

This book you now hold in your hands is the fruit of divine inspiration, long experience, and the steady labor of love and faith. It is not merely a collection of ideas or methods, but the overflow of a life surrendered to God's purpose and refined through years of faithful obedience. For as long as I have known her, my wife has carried a deep and genuine love for God, for children, and for teaching—paired with a Spirit-given commitment to excellence in all she does. It has been my great privilege to watch that love mature, deepen, and take shape through patience, discipline, and tireless devotion to growth.

Over the years, I have seen her submit herself to the often-unseen process of development. Like many, she learned that gifts and talents, though divinely given, begin as potential rather than polish. They are raw in form—like a diamond in the rough—requiring extraction, shaping, and refinement before their full value can be revealed. God-given ability does not mature automatically; it must be trained, practiced, and stewarded with intentionality. This book was born out of that realization and out of a sincere desire to honor God by serving others with wisdom, clarity, and truth.

Scripture reminds us of the importance of this responsibility. Proverbs 22:6 instructs us to "train up a child in the way he should go, and when he is old, he will not depart from it." Training is not incidental; it is foundational. Whether we recognize it or not, each of us has been shaped—both positively and negatively—by those who invested in us, instructed us, and modeled life before us. Developmental training matters because formation always precedes function.

The Scriptures give us a powerful example of this truth in the life of Samuel. In the book of First Samuel, we see a young boy who would become Israel's last judge and one of its greatest prophets. Samuel's prophetic calling did not emerge in isolation; it was discovered, nurtured, and developed from an early age. He had parents who understood the value of dedication, and mentors who helped him recognize and respond to the voice of God. His life illustrates an essential principle: when a gift is discovered, the next critical question is how it will be trained and strengthened.

Training begins with awareness, but it must be followed by practice. Without guidance, even sincere passion can remain unfocused. This book provides language, structure, and practical tools designed to help both the young and the mature grow in prophetic understanding and expression. It bridges spiritual sensitivity with responsible instruction, ensuring that gifting is developed in a way that honors God and edifies others.

My prayer is that these pages serve as a trustworthy guide on your journey—helping you recognize God's work, cultivate what He has entrusted to you, and walk forward with confidence, humility, and purpose. May God bless your growth, your training, and your pursuit of His voice.

Elder Antonio January

# DEDICATIONS

To Antonio, my husband, my biggest supporter, the one who runs with every idea the Lord gives me and cheers me on.

To Elizabeth (Liz) Fitch, my friend, my encourager, my destiny helper. This work wouldn't have happened without you. Your legacy shall live on.

To my very own dreamers and seers Love, Je'Taime, Gabrielle and Savannah. May you stand on my shoulders and see further, deeper and higher than I could ever see. Stay rooted and grounded in your relationship with God and the Word.

# INTRODUCTION

At the age of nine years old I fell in love with Jesus. I remember wanting to be baptized, profess His name and learn all I could about Him in Sunday School. I could not get enough of Him. From that point on I would have prophetic dreams, visions and angelic encounters. I remember after tarrying for Holy Spirit an angel was standing in front of me. It was so tall, all I could see was the wing. I could hear the sound of a wing flapping. My life was forever changed.  I would try to explain my dreams and visions to my elders but they did not understand or they would ask me not to talk about it. Some would say, "What a gift you have!" But that was as far as it would go.  I had no one around me to mentor me or give me language to the gift I have so I kept these experiences between me and God in my journal.

UNTIL right before COVID in March 2020, I had a dream that my friend lost her job. The dream was very detailed. She sent me a text that read, "I just lost my job." At the time she was the breadwinner for her family.  As soon as I woke up I began to intercede for her that she would not lose her job because her family needs her. Two weeks later my friend texted me and it read, "I just lost my job." It happened the same way I dreamt it. I sat down immediately and began to pray again. A few hours later my friend got her job back. That experience shook me and I prayed that the Holy Spirit would lead me to develop this gift and to use it for His glory. So, I did what most millennials do when they want to learn something. I went to YouTube University. I came across Apostles Tomi Arayaomi and Tobi Arayomi. Their testimonies and knowledge of the Word of God was like nothing I have ever seen before. Also, I am a twin and I have identical twin daughters so the twin dynamic was so cool to me. I was all in. I would binge watch hours of their old videos and take notes.

One day I heard Apostle Tomi share the vision/words that the Lord gave him for RIG Nation. Training seven thousand prophets. I thought, "Meh, I think I am prophetic, but I do not know if this is for me but I will give it a shot. What do I have to lose? Liz also encouraged me to take the class. She was a 2021 Master Class graduate. I signed up for Master Class 2022 and by the second class I thought, "I don't belong here. This class isn't for me." I was intimidated. As soon as I had that thought Apostle Tomi said, "If you don't think you belong here, you do." That was all I needed to hear to press on. I am so glad I did. I graduated from RIG School of Apostles & Prophets Masterclass 2022 and RIG School of Apostles and Prophets Train the Trainer in 2023. In order to graduate we had to write a thesis to prove we have the knowledge of what was being taught and what we were going to do with what we learned. I asked Holy Spirit to reveal to me what I was supposed to do with what I learned. Holy Spirit led me to create a curriculum for youth. That word was confirmed by at least four people. This work is a result of obedience to God. May it richly bless the youth and elders alike.

**Summary**: Do you long to understand your dreams, recognize divine visions, walk confidently in your prophetic purpose and/or teach your children and young students to do the same? In 37: Hands-On Biblical Lessons That Activate the Dreamer and Seer Within. Montia January guides teachers and students through a spirit-led journey inspired by Genesis 37 and Ezekiel 37 - two chapters that reveal how God births destiny through dreams and breathes life into dry places. This hands-on curriculum blends biblical study, reflection and prophetic activations to help you:

- Interpret dreams and visions using Scripture.

- Recognize God's voice and symbolism.

- Strengthen your discernment through practical exercises.

- Partner with the Holy Spirit in everyday life.

Whether for personal growth, small group study, Bible Study or ministry training, 37 will equip and inspire you to live as a believer, seer and/or dreamer who walks in revelation and power.

**How to use this curriculum:**

1. 37 can be used at home, in bible studies, small groups, Sunday School and even individually.

2. Lessons 1-11 are very hands-on and can be used for ages 3+ - adulthood.

3. Lessons 12-37 are a little more advanced and have more scriptures. You know your children/students better than I do. I suggest reading the lessons ahead of time and modifying them for your age group while not underestimating your children/students.

4. At the end of each lesson is a note section for you to add your impressions, more scriptures or ways to make the lessons your own.

**Objectives:**

1. That children and young adults will know God, His thoughts, His ways, His Spirit, His Word and how to flow with Him.

2. That children will utilize the gifts, talents and abilities that God has given them and use them for His glory.

3. That children will know the voice of the Lord and share His word with others.

4. That children will learn to exercise/train their spiritual senses. Hebrews 5:14 NKJV - But solid food belongs to those who are of full age, that is, those who by reason of use have their senses exercised to discern both good and evil.

**Tools:**

Bible Journal Sketchbook

Writing Utensils

Dream Dictionary: The Divinity Code to Understanding Your Dreams and Visions by Adam F. Thompson and Adrian Beale or A to Z Dream Symbology Dictionary by Dr. Barbie L. Breathitt (optional).

**Important Guidelines for Teachers:**

1. Begin each lesson with prayer and soaking worship music.

2. Pray for each student. Ask the Holy Spirit to reveal to you each child's gift.

3. Pray over each lesson and prepare days in advance. Don't prepare the day of the lesson.

4. Always be a student.

5. Always leave room for the Holy Spirit when you teach.

**Basic Introduction of Dreams**

1. Only use the Holy Spirit and the Word of God to interpret dreams.

Genesis 40:8 - And they said to him, "We each have had a dream, and there is no interpreter of it." So Joseph said to them, "Do not interpretations belong to God? Tell them to me, please.

2. Lessons we can learn from Joseph according to the Kingdom Dynamics: "Joseph held the vision God gave him for his life. It kept him through everything he experienced. He was restrained from sin, redeemed from sorrow, and restored to honor by holding on to the dreams from God. Here are five guidelines we learn from Joseph.

    a. RECEIVE God's promise with child-like faith (Genesis 37: 5-10).

    b. MAKE the best of bad situations (Genesis 39: 4, 12).

    c. STAND with integrity in trials and temptations.

    d. WALK in humility before God (Genesis 41: 14-57).

    e. SEE everything in life from God's perspective (Genesis 45 - Genesis 50:20). New Spirit-Filled Bible, NKJV. Thomas-Nelson. 2552. p58.

3. Where do dreams come from?

    a. From God (divine dreams). The purpose of divine dreams are to guide, reveal truth, confirm direction, or warn for protection. (Genesis 37, Genesis 41 and Matthew 2:13).

b. From the soul (self/natural dreams). Soulish dreams come from your own thoughts, emotions, and experiences. They expose what is on your heart and mind. (Ecclesiastes 5:3).

c. The enemy (demonic dreams). Demonic dreams are fear-based or deceptive dreams designed to plant confusion, fear or distraction. (Jeremiah 23:25-32).

# OLD TESTAMENT

## JOSEPH: THE DREAMER

1. Welcome and open in prayer.

2. Introduction: Joseph the Dreamer. Text: Genesis 37: 6-11

3. What do we notice about the dream?

4. Symbols in the dream (sheaves, sun, moon, stars). Dream dictionaries can help to interpret your dreams. It is also important to ask the Holy Spirit to give you wisdom.

5. "A dream confirms God's providence. He is acting through Joseph." (Spirit-Filled Life Bible. NKJV. Nelson. Providence = the protective care or spiritual care of God.

   a. The teacher could give an example of a protective dream they had. I had a dream at the beginning of the 2020 pandemic that my home was surrounded by a big fence and my neighbor's dog ZuZu was walking around it.

      i. What symbols do you notice in this dream? Fence and Dog

      ii. What does a fence do? Fence = protection

      iii. What does a dog do? Dog = Guard Dog

      iv. Interpretation = God was showing me in my dream that He was going to keep my home/family safe from COVID and indeed He did. I was afraid of COVID, we feared the unknown but the Lord showed us that He was going to protect our home.

6. Who wants to share a dream that we can interpret?

7. Any Questions? (Always allow time for the students to ask questions).

Memory Verse: Genesis 40:8 - And they said to him, "We each have had a dream, and there is no interpreter of it." So Joseph said to them, "Do not interpretations belong to God? Tell them to me, please.

**Note:**

Kingdom Dynamics: Genesis 37:5 "Rooted to a Dream, prophetic dreams and visions. The Hebrew word for "had a dream" means to bind firmly (Strongs #2492). Joseph became firmly bound up in the dream that God had given him. Dreams that are from God are spiritual experiences that root deep in our hearts, never to be forgotten. Joseph had a dream but more accurately we could say that the dream had Joseph! The dream sustained him through all that happened to him throughout the years," (New Spirit Filled Life Bible, NKJV, Nelson 2552, p.54).

# Notes

# THE CHIEF BUTLER'S DREAM

Teacher Note: Before introducing this lesson, have a recap of last week's lesson to refresh the students memories and to help students catch up who may not have been in attendance.

1. Welcome and open in prayer.

2. Introduction: Chief Butler's Dream. Text Genesis 40:1-15

   a. Ask the students what do they notice from this passage of scripture?

   b. Important: Joseph was sensitive to the needs of others (he noticed the prisoners were sad. Joseph also gave glory to God)

   c. What are the symbols in the dream? (vines, cup, grapes)

   d. Numbers can be symbolic #3 is in this dream. (If you have a dream dictionary show them how to look it up).

3. Does anyone have a dream they would like to share?

4. Does any student have any questions?

5. Close out in prayer.

# Notes

# PHARAOH'S DREAM

1. Welcome and open in prayer.

   a. Recap last week's lesson.

2. Introduction: We are going to break down another dream that Joseph interpreted.

   a. Text: Genesis 41: 1-32 (ask for volunteers to read).

   b. Memory Verse 41:16 So, Joseph answered Pharoah and said, "It is not in me, God will give Pharaoh an answer of peace."

3. Questions: What symbols are in the dream? (thin cows, fat cows, number seven, good grain and thin grain.)

   a. What did Joseph say the cows and grain represent? (seven years of plenty). What happens when you have plenty of food? (you gain weight)

   b. What did Joseph say the thin grains and cow represent (seven years of famine = prolonged hunger). What happens when you don't eat a lot of food? (You lose weight. You get thin.)

   c. Why do you think the Pharaoh had the dream twice? Genesis 41: 32 And the dream was repeated to Pharaoh twice because the thing was established by God, and God will shortly bring it to pass. **This is an example of a repetitive dream.**

4. Ask the students if they have any questions.

5. Ask the students if they have any dreams they would like to share.

6. Homework: Bring a dream to class and we will practice interpreting the dream.

7. Close in prayer

# Notes

# PRACTICAL DREAM INTERPRETATION I

1.  Welcome and pen with prayer.

    a.  Ask for a recap from last week's lesson.

2.  Who brought a dream to interpret?

3.  What are the keys to remember when interpreting a dream?

    a.  R = remember to pray and ask God for the interpretation of the dream.

    b.  O = only decode one line at a time.

    c.  Y = yield (wait) for the interpretation to come. You might receive a word, a scripture, a song, a memory, a sound, a vision, etc.)

    d.  G = get a pen and paper and write. Revelation may come by what you write.

    e.  B = be prepared to ask the dreamer questions: how did you feel, what colors did you see, could you smell or taste anything, what does the symbols mean to you (sometimes the symbols are only relevant to the dreamer).

    f.  P = prophesy by interpreting the dream. When you interpret the dream, you are in essence prophesying.

4.  Choose a student's dream to interpret. You may have time to interpret more than one. Work on the interpretation as a group.

5.  Before closing, ask if anyone has any questions?

6.  Close in prayer.

# Notes

# SIX THINGS DREAMS DO

1. Welcome and Open in prayer/

   a. Ask the students to give a recap of last week's lesson.

2. Introduce Gideon to the class. Read the text: Judges 7: 9-15. In essence, God gave Gideon instructions but he was afraid. However, God sent confirmation through a dream that someone else had, that what God said will come to pass.

3. "What are the six things that dreams do?

   a. Provides God's answers to our questions as in this text.

   b. Instruct us in the things of God. Matthew 1:19-21 (read it or ask for volunteers to read the scriptures).

   c. Warn us about unseen dangers. Matthew 2:12, 13, 22.

   d. Guide us away from wrongdoing. Genesis 20:3-8.

   e. Keep us from pride. Daniel 4: 19-37.

   f. Save our lives. Matthew 2:13." (New Spirit-Filled Bible, NKJV, Thomas - Nelson. 2552. p. 325).

4. Ask students if they have an example of a dream that was an instruction, warning, guide, kept them from pride or saved them. If they do not, provide an example. (The teacher can give an example if the students don't have one).

5. Close in prayer.

# Notes

# PROPHETIC ART - DRAWING

Items Needed:

- Crayons, Pencils or Markers

- Soaking Worship Music

Activation:

1. Welcome and Open in Prayer

2. Invite the children to close their eyes and imagine what Jesus looks like.

   a. Have them draw a picture of what they saw.

   b. When they are done drawing Him, have them share their pictures and talk about them as a group.

3. Follow up with the text: Revelation 19: 11-16 and Revelation 1:9-20

4. Ask the children if they have any questions.

5. Close in prayer.

6. Encourage them to keep their drawings in their journals.

# Notes

# PROPHETIC ART 2 - PAINTING & DESIGN

Items Needed:

- Canvases

- Paint/Paintbrushes

- Art Smocks or Old Tshirts

- Soaking Worship Music

1. Welcome and Opening Prayer.

    a. Ask the children to recap last week's lesson.

2. Explain to the children that this lesson is similar to last week's lesson but this time we're going to paint whatever we hear and see. Whatever vision or word is pressed upon us. There is no right or wrong image.

3. Questions:

    a. Who enjoys painting?

    b. Does anyone know of or think that there are any artists in the Bible?

    c. Text: Exodus 31: 1-5

    d. Artisans = a worker in a skilled trade, especially one that involves making things by hand.

4. When the children are done, ask them to share their paintings and discuss them.

5. Ask if the children have any questions.

6. Close in prayer.

# Notes

# PROPHETIC ART 3 - MUSIC

Items needed:

- Dance scarves

- Tambourines

- Soaking Worship Music/Speaker

- Journals

- Shofar (optional)

1. **Welcome and Opening Prayer**: Ask someone to lead prayer.

    a. Have a recap of what happened last week.

    b. Give a summary of who David is. Yes, he is a giant killer but he is also a poet and hymnodist (a person who writes texts or songs). He wrote most of the book of Psalms.

    c. Read II Samuel 6:14-16 - Then David danced before the Lord with all his might; and David was wearing a linen ephod. So David and all the house of Israel brought up the ark of the Lord with shouting and with the sound of the trumpet.

2. **Activation:**

    a. Play, "I'm Not Ashamed," by Free Chapel. Give the students dance scarves and invite them to dance before the Lord. Some children may be reluctant but that is ok. Don't make them dance. Invite them to worship the way they want to.

b. Play your favorite soaking worship song or "Shofar Intercession Instrumental" by Kyle Lovett. Blow your shofar if you have one. Have the students dance or sit still before the Lord and journal.

c. Afterwards have the students journal their experience (what did they feel, what did they hear). Invite them to share if they want to.

3. **Closing:**

a. Recap about David and dancing before the Lord.

b. Ask the students if they have any questions.

c. Have a student close in prayer.

d. Always leave space for Holy Spirit.

# Notes

# PROPHETIC JOURNALING - POEMS/HYMNS: GOD & NATURE

Items Needed:

- Bibles

- Journals

- Speakers/Music

- Notes: If weather permits, this lesson could be done outside. Additional items that would be needed are:

  - Blankets and chairs

1. Welcome and open in prayer.

2. Recap last week's lesson.

   a. David

   b. What are psalms?

3. Introduction to this week's lesson: God and Nature

   a. Ask the students what they think about God and Nature.

   b. Read or have a student read Psalm 8. This Psalm is titled as, "The Glory of the Lord in Creation," written by David.

   c. Words that may need to be defined: glory, honor, son of man.

   d. Ask the students their thoughts on Psalm 8. Does anything surprise them, make them think, or is brand new to them.

e. **Objective**: Students will ponder God's creation and what creation says about who God is. Students will journal and write what they believe God is saying about them.

f. **Activation** : Journaling Scripture: Psalm 8:4 - What is man that you are mindful of him, and the son of man that you visit him? (visit him = to take care of Him).

g. Give the students 10-15 to journal. When they are done ask anyone if they would like to share.

h. Closing

    i. Any questions?

    ii. Prayer

# Notes

# PROPHETIC JOURNALING (POEMS/HYMNS): GOD & NATURE

(This is another lesson that would be great to complete outside). Items Needed:

- Bible

- Speaker/Music (Soaking Worship Song w/ Water)

- Journals

1. Welcome and Open in Prayer (ask for any volunteers).

2. Recap last week's lesson.

3. Introduce this week's lesson. We're still learning about God and nature. Psalm

23. One of the most well-known passages of scripture is Psalm 23. It is written by David and is titled, "The Lord the Shepherd of His People."

4. Ask for a volunteer to read Psalm 23.

5. Ask the students how this passage of scripture makes them feel.

a. Has anyone ever been comforted by the Lord? What did it feel like?

6. **Activation - Spontaneous Praise** - invite the students to lay on their blanket and read the passage of scripture again. Ask the students to journal what they sense; taste, feel, hear, see, and smell. (10-20 minutes). If students can't write they can draw pictures.

7. **Objective** - Students will learn to discern/activate their senses by journaling what they sense.

8.  Closing

    a.  Any questions, comments, concerns?

    b.  Anyone want to share about what they sensed?

    c.  Prayer.

# Notes

# TASTE AND SEE!

Items Needed:

- Bible

- Journals

- Speaker/Music

1. Welcome and Opening Prayer

   a. Prayer - ask for a volunteer

   b. Recap of last week's lesson.

2. Introducing lesson: Taste and See. Psalm 34: 1- 8

   a. Ask for volunteer to read it.

   b. Define taste = (ta'am) discern, eat, perceive, evaluate, testing by good by means of sense of taste.

3. **Activation** - What is your partner's favorite food.

   a. Pair up the students.

   b. Pray in the spirit for a few minutes.

   c. Pray that the Holy Spirit reveals to each student what each other's favorite food is by what they taste.

   d. Have each child write it down in their journals and then share with the class.

4. **Objective** - students will learn that the Holy Spirit can use each of our senses to tell us about someone so that we can prophesy to them (tell them what the Lord says).

5. **Closing**

    a.  How did that activation make you feel?

    b.  Any questions?

    c.  Prayer

# Notes

# DREAM DREAMS AND SEE VISIONS

Items Needed:

- Bible with a Concordance

- Speaker: Prophetic Soaking Music

- Journals

- Strong's Concordance (optional)

- Dream Dictionary (optional)

- Song: I Prophesy, Brandon Lake

1. **Welcome and Opening Prayer**

    a. Worship

    b. Recap of last week

2. **Introduction of This Week's Lesson: Dream Dreams and See Visions**

    c. Scripture: Joel 2:28 - And it shall come to pass afterward that I will pour out my Spirit upon all flesh; and your sons and your daughters shall prophesy, your old men shall dream dreams and your young men shall see visions.

    d. Questions:

        i. How many of you have had a vision from the Lord? What was the vision? Describe your experience. Personal note: Share my vision of the angel when I was tarrying for Holy Spirit when I first got saved.Teacher note: Share any visions the Lord gave you.

ii. Why do you think God gives us visions? (Visions can give us faith and hope. They can also warn us). What is a vision? Supernatural revelation or divine communication from God, often given while a person is awake. It's how God makes His will, plans, or messages known beyond ordinary sight or understanding.

iii. Visions are initiated by God, not by human imagination.

iv. Visions allows a person to see into the spiritual realm (angels, future events or God's glory). Isaiah 6:1 - I saw the Lord sitting upon a throne, high and lifted up.

e. Today we are going to learn about Ezekial. His name means "God Strengthens or God is strong."

i. He had six visions from God that were very symbolic. James Goll said, "If you want to have more visions from the Lord, study the book of Ezekiel."

ii. Read Ezekiel 1:1-21

iii. We are going to break the vision down in three parts

1. Ezekiel 1:4-14: The Storm and the Creatures (this week)

2. Ezekiel 1:15-21: Wheel and the Glory of God (next week)

3. Ezekiel 1:22-28: The Firmament and the Throne (the following week)

iv. Ask for a volunteer to read Ezekiel 1:4-14 and encourage the rest of the class to write down the symbols they notice in their journals. (whirlwind, cloud, fire, living creatures, four faces, …

f. How to interpret visions?

i. Always pray and ask Holy Spirit to help.

ii.   Use your concordance at the back of your Bible for help or the Strong's Concordance to look up meanings of words. (Show them an example.)

iii.  Other biblical references.

3. **Objective - Students Will Learn How to Interpret Some Symbols In Visions.**

4. **Application**

g.  What do you think the whirlwind represents? (God) We will interpret these symbols together.

   i.   Concordance 2 Kings 2:1 And it came to pass when the Lord was about to take up Elijah into heaven by a whirlwind that Elijah went with Elijah to Gilgal.

h.  What do you think the four living creatures represent? Do you think the four are symbolic?

   i.   The number four in this chapter represents completeness. It is used 12 times in this chapter and 40 times in the Bible. (Have students look up the following chapters.

1. Ezekiel 37:9 - the four winds

2. Genesis 13:14 - four directions

3. Isaiah 11:12 - four corners

   ii.  Question: Let's think about in our world, things that are governed by the number four. Who can tell me?

1. Seasons: Fall, Winter, Summer and Spring

2. Directions: North, South, East and West.

   iii.  The creatures are cherubim.

   iv.  Important note: It is vital to depend on Holy Spirit to interpret visions. "Ezekiel tries to use the known to describe the unknown.

5. **Objective - Students Will Learn How to Interpret Numbers And Symbols In Visions.**

6. **ACTIVATION - ASK GOD FOR A VISION**

    i.   Pray in the spirit for a few minutes.

    j.   Ask God to give you a vision.

    k.   Journal or draw what the Lord showed you.

    l.   Share as a class.

    m.   Deeper thought: ask God for a scripture that goes with the vision.

7. **Closing (Questions and Prayers)**

8. **Homework: Study and meditate on Ezekiel 1. Come Back Next Week with Any Questions or Revelations About the Chapter.**

# Notes

# DREAM DREAMS AND SEE VISIONS 2

Items Needed:

- Bible with a Concordance

- Speaker: Prophetic Soaking Music

- Journals

- Strong's Concordance (optional)

- Dream Dictionary (optional)

- Song: I Prophesy, Brandon Lake

1. **Welcome and Opening Prayer**

   a. Who did their homework?

   b. Who would like to share any revelations the Lord gave them about Ezekiel Chapter One?

2. **Introduction and Recap**

   c. Who can tell me what the number four means?

   d. What's the name of the four creatures?

   e. Lesson text: Ezekiel 1:15-21. We are continuing to discuss how to interpret visions. Ask for a volunteer to read the scripture.

3. **Application**

   f. What do you think the wheels mean?

g.  What do you think the eyes mean? (God's all-seeing nature).

h.  The whole description seems to symbolize the omnipresence of God. He is capable of moving in any direction.

i.  Questions: What stood out to you in these verses?

j.  Who knows what omnipresence is?

k.  Omnipotent (unlimited power). Omniscient (knows everything). Omnipresent (ability to be everywhere all at once).

4.  **Objective - Students Will Learn the Meaning of Basic Symbols In Dreams.**

5.  **Activation - Ask God for A Vision for Your Partner.**

    l.  Pray in the spirit for a few minutes.

    m.  Ask God to give you a vision for your partner. Draw it or write it in your journal.

    n.  Share the visions with the class.

    o.  Deeper thinking: Ask the Lord for a scripture with the vision and pray over your partner.

6.  **Closing**

    p.  Any questions

    q.  Homework - read Ezekiel Chapter 1:22-28

    r.  Prayer

# Notes

# DREAM DREAMS AND SEE VISIONS 3

Items Needed:

- Bible with a Concordance

- Speaker: Prophetic Soaking Music

- Journals

- Strong's Concordance (optional)

- Dream Dictionary (optional)

- Song: I Prophesy, Brandon Lake

1. **Opening** (prayer, who did their homework and has any questions or revelations)

2. **Introduction and Recap**

   a. What do the eyes represent in the text from last week?

   b. What are the three O-words we talked about and what do they mean?

   c. We are going to close out Ezekiel Chapter 1. Who would like to volunteer to read?

3. **Lesson Text**

   d. Ezekiel 1:22-28

   e. What is a firmament? (The same word used for Heaven in Genesis 1: 6-8 NKJV.)  Then God said let there be firmament in the midst of the waters, and let it divide the waters from the waters. Thus God made the firmament and divided the waters which were under the firmament from the waters which were above the firmament; and it was so. And God called the firmament Heaven. So the evening and the morning were the second day.

    f.   Definition - In the Bible, the firmament is a solid dome that God created to separate the primal sea into upper and lower portions, allowing dry land to appear. Hebrew Word = raqia (rakeeah)." (Wikipedia) Provide a visual for visual learners.

    g.   This is what I would call a straight-forward vision. There isn't anything to interpret. What you see is what you get.

    h.   Ezekiel was receiving a vision of God.

4. **Objective - Students Will Learn That Some Visions Are Straight Forward and Doesn't Need to Be Interpreted.**

5. **Application/Questions**

    a.   Have you ever seen the glory of the Lord?

    b.   Personal Note: Retell your angel story. Teachers: Share your story of if you've ever seen the glory of the Lord or have felt the wind of God.

6. **Activation - Lord, Show Me Your Glory.**

    c.   Pray in the spirit. Put on soaking worship music. This will be one-on-one time. Ask God to show you His glory.

    d.   Write or draw what you see.

7. **Closing (Prayer, Questions, Homework - Spend Time in Your Secret Place With God 15 - 30 Minutes Longer Than You Normally Do).**

# Notes

# PROPHESY TO THE DRY BONES

Items Needed:

- Bible with a Concordance

- Speaker: Prophetic Soaking Music

- Journals

- Strong's Concordance (optional)

- Dream Dictionary (optional)

- Song: I Prophesy, Brandon Lake

1. **Opening** (welcome, prayer, discuss homework - who spent time in the secret place, how did it go, what did they discover, any questions or revelations).

2. **Introduction and Recap**

   a. What did we discuss last week?

   b. What is a firmament?

   c. What is a divine vision?

3. **Lesson Text**

a. Ezekiel 37 1:14

   b. Breath = Hebrew = ruah and can be translated breath, wind or spirit. There is constant word play in verses 7-10, 14.

4. **Objective** - students will learn how to release a prophetic word to people and what word play means.

5. **Application/Questions**

    a. Give an example of word play. Trudy - Trudy My Trooper.

6. **Activation - Prophesy to the Breath.**

    a. Give 10-15 minutes for this activation. Play soaking worship music.

    b. Assign partners. Have the partners prophesy about something that may be laying dormant in their partners life or something they are worried about. Then pray into it.

    c. Stretch - what is God declaring over your partner's life. Make declarations.

7. **Homework** - Study Ezekiel 37. Pray over your partner you prophesied to.

# PROPHESY TO THE NATIONS
# (GROUP ACTIVATION)

Items Needed:

- Bible with a Concordance

- Speaker: Prophetic Soaking Music

- Journals

- Large Tongue Dispensers

- Fine point markers

- Map or Globe

1. **Welcome and Opening Prayer**

   a. Ask a volunteer to recap of last week's lesson

   b. Who did their homework, anything to share, any revelations?

2. **Introduction**

   a. Text - Ezekiel 37:15-28 - Ask for a volunteer to read it.

   b. Lesson Title - Prophesying to the Nations

   c. Ezekiel 37:16 - each piece of wood symbolized one kingdom.

   d. God wants to bring all these nations together and be their God.

e. God is a God of the nations. There are some nations that don't know about God at all. It is important to pray for other nations, especially the one we live in.

   i. Matthew 24:14

3. **Objective** - students will learn how to release a prophetic word for nations.

4. **Activation**

   a. Each student will spin the globe. Where their finger stops on the globe is the nation they will pray for.

      i. Write the name of the nation of your stick.

      ii. As you pray, ask for a word, declaration or vision for the nation. Ask God what He is doing in that nation. Write it in your journal and on your stick. (If younger children are in the room that can't write, they can draw pictures of what they see).

      iii. We will come together as a group to discuss what we received from the Lord.

      iv. If time permits we will research some of the nations.

5. **Homework** - pray over the nation you were given. Research the nation and pray for their souls to be saved. Pray for the Christians that are already in that nation.

# Notes

# PROPHESY TO THE FAMILIES

Items Needed:

- Bible with a Concordance

- Speaker: Prophetic Soaking Music

- Journals

- Large Tongue Dispensers

- Fine point markers

1. **Welcome and Opening Prayer**

   a.  Ask a volunteer to recap of last week's lesson

   b.  Who did their homework, anything to share, any revelations?

2. **Introduction**

   a.  Text - Ezekiel 37:15-28 - Ask for a volunteer to read it.

   b.  Lesson Title - Prophesying to Families

   c.  Ezekiel 37:16 - each piece of wood symbolized one kingdom.

   d.  God wants to bring families together and be their God.

   e.  God is a God of families. There are some family members that don't know about God.

      i.  Ezekiel 37:18 - And when the children of your people speak to you, saying, "Will you not show us what you mean by these?" NKJV

3. **Objective** - students will learn how to release a prophetic word for families.

4. **Activation**

    a. Each student will write their last name on a stick. Place the sticks in a bag.

    b. Have each student grab a stick.

    c. Pray over the family and ask the Lord for a prophetic word/vision and declaration for the family. Journal the word. Release the word.

    d. We will pray together for each family.

5. **Homework** - pray over the families that God gave you a prophetic word for.

# Notes

# WALK INTO THE RIVER - EZEKIEL 47:1-12

Items Needed:

Bible Journals

Music (Soaking Worship Music with Water) Healing Rivers Flow by Terri Geisel

1. **Welcome And Opening Prayer**

    a. Ask for a volunteer to recap last week's lesson.

    b. Who did their homework? Anything to share? Any testimonies?

2. **Introduction**

    a. Lesson Title: Walk Into The River

    b. Ask for a volunteer to read Ezekiel 47: 1-12

    c. Ask the students what stands out to them in this scripture and why?

    d. Define what river symbolizes which is the… "ability to flow in and follow the leading of the Holy Spirit." Dr. Barbie L. Breathitt

    e. Other passages of scripture where this river is found; Revelations 22:1, Joel 3:18 and Zechariah 14:8.

3. **Objective** - students will learn to activate their spiritual senses.

4. **Activation** (Walk into the River)

    a. Play soaking worship music and read Ezekiel 47:1-12 again.

    b. Pray and ask the Lord: What do you want me to see in the river? Vs. 6: Son of man, have you seen this? What are you doing in the river? Journal what you feel, see, hear, taste and smell.

c.  Ask for volunteers to share with the group.

5. **Homework**: Use your concordance to find scriptures in the Bible about rivers. Write them in your journal and bring them next week to share with the class.

# Notes

# WALK INTO THE RIVER II

Items Needed:

Bible

Journals

Music (Suggestion: Sondae, Deeper)

1. **Welcome And Opening Prayer**

    a.  Ask for a volunteer to recap last week's lesson.

    b.  Ask for a volunteer to share their homework.

2. **Introduction: Walk Into the River II (Repetition Deepens the Impression).**

    a.  Ask for a volunteer to read Ezekiel 47: 1-12.

    b.  Ask if anything stands out now that did not stand out last week.

    c.  As new testament believers we have two exciting and uniquely wonderful opportunities. This is the first look forward in faith to the heavenly temple. From it flows the river of God whose waters bring life and healing to everything they touch. The second is to understand that we can walk in the river of God now. We have within us the Holy Spirit and God's resurrection power. The Lord desires to use us as instruments of healing to the nations to extend His healing to everything we touch." (Commentary from New Spirit Life Filled Bible. p1116)

3. **Objective** - students will learn how to activate their spiritual senses.

4.  **Activation: Walk Into the River II**

    a.  "Ezekiel gives a picture of walking steadily deeper into the river until, by his own strength, he could no longer navigate the current. We are to walk increasingly deeper in the Holy Spirit, releasing ourselves entirely to Him. Ask the Lord to take you deeper in the power and anointing of the Holy Spirit." (Commentary New Spirit Life Filled Bible. p.1116).

    b.  Assign partners and ask the Lord to reveal to you what He is bringing your partner out of so that they can go deeper in Him. Journal it. Share it. Pray over it. Declare it.

    c.  Ask for volunteers to share with the group.

5.  **Homework** - pray for your partner to go deeper in the Lord.

# Notes

# WHAT DO YOU SEE

Items Needed:

Bibles Journals

Soaking Worship Music

1. **Welcome and Opening Prayer**

   a. Ask for a volunteer to recap last week's lesson. Does anyone have any thoughts or questions?

   b. Ask a volunteer to share if they did their homework.

2. **Introduction - What Do You See - Jeremiah 1:1-13**

   a. Ask for a volunteer to read Jeremiah 1:1-12.

   b. Does anything resonate with you in this passage of scripture?

   c. Highlight vs 6-8 (read them again).

      i. Jeremiah thought that because he was a youth, he could not speak. God being with you will help you to overcome your insecurities.

      ii. Three things God demanded of Jeremiah; stop voicing your disqualifications, speak obediently, and refuse to fear.

      iii. God trained Jeremiah Himself. Jeremiah 1:11-12 (read it). What do you notice here? Any symbols (the almond tree).

God gave Jeremiah a vision. Then he said, "I am ready to perform my word."

   a. Amos 3:7 - Surely the Lord does nothing unless He reveals His secret to His servants the prophets.

b. God watches over His word to perform it.

c. Almond = watching (in Hebrew), "...it is a reminder that the almond tree blooms early in the spring, becoming the tree that is ready and watching as all other blossoms/events unfold," (9g. 959).

3. **What Can We Learn from God Training Jeremiah as A Prophet?**

   a. Parents, know that God has a purpose and plan for your unborn child. Pray for them.

   b. Say yes to the call and training for the gift of prophecy.

   c. Ask God to open your spiritual eyes to what He wants to show you.

   d. Wait and listen for God's interpretation of what you see prophetically. Often the prophetic word is in the symbol.

4. **Objective** - students will be encouraged that their age has nothing to do with their ability to see supernatural things.

5. **Activation - What Do You See**

   a. We will pray as a group for God to open our spiritual eyes and ask: Lord, what do you want to show me?

   b. Journal what you see. Then ask God for the interpretation of what you saw.

   c. Ask for volunteers to share what they saw. Encourage the students not to be discouraged if they saw one image. If they only saw one image - search it out as a symbol.

6. **Closing**

   a. Any questions, comments or concerns.

   b. Homework - read Jeremiah 1-10.

# Notes

# THE POTTER AND THE CLAY

Items Needed:

Clay or Playdough Journals

Soaking Worship Music

1. **Welcome and Opening Prayer**

   a. Ask for a volunteer to recap last week's lesson.

   b. Ask who did their homework and what was their experience.

2. **Introduction: The Potter and The Clay (Jeremiah 18:1-6)**

   a. Ask if anyone knows about this passage of scripture. Ask for a volunteer to read the passage of scripture.

   b. "Jeremiah visits the potter's house at God's command. There he learns that the potter sometimes rejected some of the pots, perhaps because of poor quality. So, God is sovereign over his people Judah. What the potter makes depends on the quality of the clay; what God makes of His people depends on their response. They clay can frustrate the potter's intention and make him alter the vessel. As the quality of the clay limits what the potter can do with it, so the quality of a people limits what God will do with them." (Commentary from New Spirit Filled Bible pg. 985).

   c. Marred = ruined. "The clay was not suitable for the potter's design. As it seemed good: He could make something else from the clay, but not the originally intended vessel," (Commentary from New Spirit Filled Bible, pg. 985).

d.  Ask your students what stands out to them the most about this passage of scripture.

3. **Objective** - students will be encouraged to be all that God has created them to be.

4. **Activation: Ask God, "What Do You Want to Make of Me?"**

   a.  Use your playdough/clay to design what God wants to make of you.

   b.  After you make your design, journal it. Then ask God if there is anything that you are doing that is keeping you from becoming that design (who He was created you to be). Journal that as well.

   c.  Ask for volunteers to share with the group.

5. **Homework** - work on what the Lord shows you that you need to change to become who He designed you to be.

# Notes

# BEWARE OF FALSE PROPHETS

Items Needed:

Bible Journals

Soaking Worship Music

1. **Welcome and Opening Prayer**

   a. Ask for a volunteer to recap last week's lesson.

   b. Ask who did their homework and if they have any questions.

2. **Introduction - False Prophets - Jeremiah 2:8-13 & Jeremiah 23:13-24**

   a. Ask for a volunteer to read the scripture.

   b. What stands out to you the most in this passage of scripture?

   c. Where do you think false visions, dreams or prophecies come from?

      i. Deceit from the human heart/imagination (Jeremiah 23:16, Ezekiel 13:2-3) = self-deception

      ii. Demonic or Lying Spirits (I Kings, 22:21-23).

      iii. False Prophets intentionally lying (Jeremiah 14:14).

   d. When we do not consult (seek the Lord) we can prophesy falsely.

      i. We can prophesy out of the desires of our hearts.

      ii. Teachers - if possible, share an example of a false prophecy.

   e. Baal = a false god; Canaanite deity. (Some references to Baal in scripture as a reference; I Kings 18, Numbers 25, Judges 6-8).

i. Baal worship was the primary spiritual threat in the old testament because it turned people away from God.

ii. Presently Baal symbolizes rebellion against the true and living God. Anything that turns you away from being devoted to God and having a demonic influence can be considered Baal.

f. During this time the prophets were prophesying what was in the people's hearts (vs 17). Not everything that is in our hearts is pure.

3. **Objective** - students will learn the characteristics of true and false prophets.

4. **Activation - Stand in The Counsel of The Lord.**

a. We're going to stand in the counsel of the Lord to receive a word, scripture or vision from the Lord. This time is between you and God. There is more than one way to stand in the counsel of the Lord.

b. Pray and ask the Lord for His counsel. Have Bibles and journals ready. Worship - don't rush the Lord.

i. Psalm 119:24 - Your statues are my delight; they are my counselors.

ii. Meditate on a scripture the Lord highlights to you.

iii. Listen and Obey. God reveals His counsel to those who are ready to act on it. Proverbs 1:23.

iv. Write what the Lord gives you.

c. Ask if anyone wants to share what they received?

5. **Homework - Stay in The Counsel of The Lord This Week.**

a. Purify your heart - live clean and humble.

b. Read and honor His Word - the Bible is your foundation.

c. Abide in His presence - prayer and worship build intimacy.

d. Listen and obey. Don't just hear, DO.

e. Surround yourself with godly voices - wise community matters.

# Notes

# FALSE REVELATIONS THROUGH DREAMS - JEREMIAH 23:25-34

Items Needed:

Bible Journal

1. **Welcome and Opening Prayer**

   a. Ask for a volunteer to recap last week's lesson.

   b. Ask if there are any revelations anyone wants to share.

2. **Introduction - False Revelations Through Dreams**

   a. Ask for a volunteer to read the scripture.

   b. Ask what stands out the most in this passage.

   c. "Usually God spoke to His prophets directly or in a vision but dreams were valid. Jeremiah rebuked the prophets for putting forth their own words as God's word, or repeating the words of others as a divine revelation from God," (New Spirit Filled Life Bible, NKJV, pg. 992).

   d. How do you know if a revelation is from the Lord and it needs to be released?

      i. As Apostle Tomi teaches, "It will feel like a burden."

      ii. Jeremiah 23:33 - oracle = burden. "There may be a wordplay. The oracle (lifting up the voice) was a burden (lifting something physically) placed upon the prophet until the message was delivered and the effect of the message was a burden for the people. On the other hand, the burden of the Lord is that the people are a burden," (New Spirit Filled Life Bible, NKJV pg. 992).

iii. Burden = Strong Concordance Definition = Massa = load, oracle, prophecy, an utterance, tribute, bearing.

iv. Other scriptures of the word burden; Malachi 1:1, Nahum 1:1, Habakkuk 1:1, Zechariah 9:1.

e. Teacher - give an example of a burden the Lord asked you to release. Ask the students if they have any examples. How did they feel? What was the outcome?

f. Teaching from COP (Company of the Prophets) - April 2, 2025.

i. Many run at the first look of what God shows them and release it. That's the presumptuous prophet (Duet. 18:20-22).

ii. Encounter your encounter. Step into your vision. Words of knowledge come when you stoop.

iii. Four dimensions of the ROEH Anointing:

1. See

2. Stoop

3. Step in

4. Scripture

iv. Revelation is always accurate. It is our interpretation of it that fails us.

3. **Activation - What Is The Oracle of The Lord That Will Profit Your Partner?**

a. Spend time praying in the spirit.

b. Ask the Lord what will profit your partner? Don't scoop off the top. See. Stoop. Step in. Scripture.

c. Journal it and share it.

Profit - The word "profit" in biblical teachings carries significant weight, extending beyond mere financial gain to encompass spiritual and moral dimensions. In the scriptures, profit is often linked with righteousness, stewardship, and the wisdom of God's provisions (www.bibledictionarytoday.com).

4. **Closing**

    a. Homework - ask the Lord to highlight someone for you to pray for (family, friend or stranger). Ask Him for a prophetic word to release over them and release it.

    b. End in prayer.

# Notes

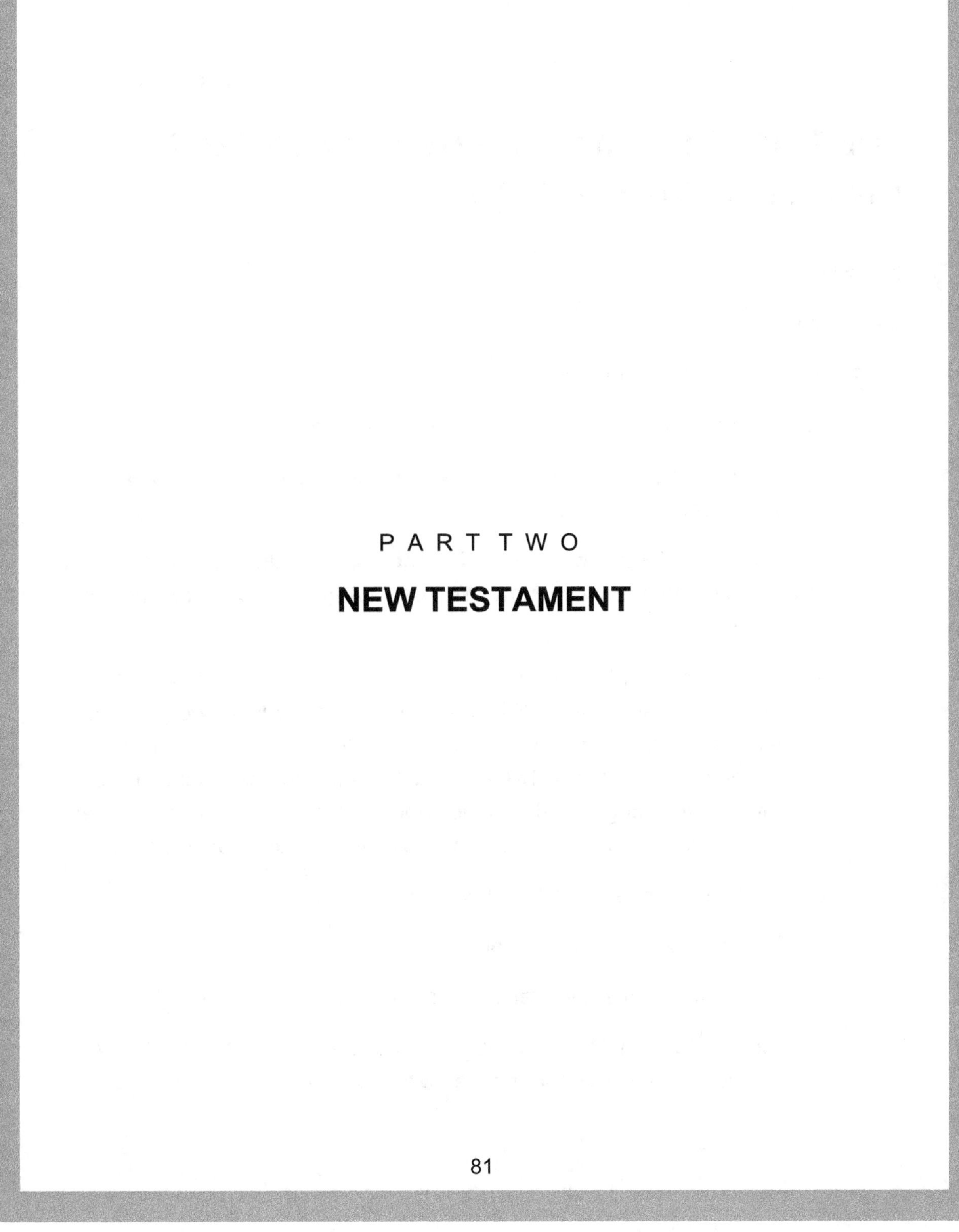

PART TWO

**NEW TESTAMENT**

# THE FIRST DREAM IN THE NEW TESTAMENT - DIVINE DIRECTION DREAM

Items Needed:

Bibles Journals

1. **Welcome and Opening Prayer**

   a. Ask for a volunteer to recap last week's lesson.

   b. Ask for a volunteer to share about what they discovered with their homework.

2. **Introduction of Part Two: We've Learned A Lot About Old Testament Dreams and Visions and Now We Are Going To Step Into The New Testament.**

   a. Who knows what the New Testament is? The second division of the Bible. It discusses the teachings and person of Jesus, as well as events relating to first century Christianity. The difference between the Old Testament and the New Testament is that the Old Testament shows us how the world began and how the people of Israel came to be. The New Testament shows us how the world is saved through Jesus Christ.

   b. Ask for someone to read the text. Matthew 1:18-25

   c. This is a divine direction dream.

      i. These dreams are straightforward and need no interpretation.

   d. Ask the students: What do you think you're supposed to do with divine direction dreams? **Teacher note: When teaching about dreams it is**

**important to emphasize that dreamers MUST steward their dreams by journaling them. Daniel 7:1b  Then he wrote down the dream, telling the main facts.**

     i.   Obey immediately. Matthew 1:24 - Then Joseph, being aroused from sleep, did as the angel of the Lord commanded him and took to him his wife.

     ii.   Write it down. It's one of the best ways to keep track of how God communicates with us and our journey with the Lord.

e.  **Important Note:** An angel of the Lord in our dreams may look like a person whose face you can't see because it is covered but they are carrying the message of the Lord. Angels are messengers from the Lord.

f.  Ask if anyone wants to share a divine direction dream?

g.  Ask if anyone has any questions.

3.  **Objective** - students will know the purpose of divine dreams.

4.  Closing Prayer - No homework. Ask students to bring their dream journals to class if they have one.

# Notes

# DIVINE WARNING DREAMS - MATTHEW 2
# THE WISE MEN AND JOSEPH

Items Needed:

Bibles Journals

1. **Welcome and Opening Prayer**

   a. Ask someone to recap last week's lesson.

   b. Where are all my dreamers? Ask who brought their dream journal to class. Later we will ask a volunteer to share a dream that we can interpret together.

2. **Three Dreams In One Chapter**

   a. Matthew 2. Ask for a volunteer to read it.

   b. Dreams vs. 12 (warning dream), 13 (warning and direction), 19 (direction).

   c. Matthew 2:12 - Then, being divinely warned in a dream that they should not return to Herod, they departed for their own country another way.

   d. Dreams are ways God communicates to people.

   e. What stands out to you the most in this chapter?

   f. Who has had divine warning or direction dreams and would like to share them? What did you learn? What was the outcome?

   g. Ask for volunteers to share some dreams from their journal.

i.  Pray for the interpretation.

ii.  Determine if it is a God dream, soulish dream or from the enemy.

3.  **Objective** - students will know what warning dreams are.

4.  **Closing**

a.  Ask if there are any more questions.

b.  No homework. Bring your journals again next week.

c.  Ask for a volunteer to close in prayer.

# Notes

# DREAMS FOR UNBELIEVERS - PILATES WIFE

Items Needed:

Bibles Journals

1. **Welcome and Opening Prayer**

   a. Ask for a volunteer to recap last week.

   b. Ask who brought their dream journal to class. We will interpret dreams later.

2. **Question: Do You Think That God Gives Dreams to Unbelievers? If So, Why or Why Not? (Allow Several Students to Answer).**

   a. Do you have any examples in the Bible of God giving unbelievers a dream?

   b. Pilate's Wife - Read or ask for a volunteer. Matthew 27: 15-26.

   c. Why do you think Pilate's wife received the dream?

      i. God can/will reveal the truth to unbelievers to save them.

      ii. God gives dreams to unbelievers to speak, warn, guide and reveal Himself.

      iii. Sometimes God uses dreams to draw people to Himself and/or position His people to interpret His message. We talked about Joseph (Genesis 37) but let's use Daniel as an example.

3. Read Daniel 2 (or summarize it because it is very long).

4.  Key verse: Daniel 2:47 - The king answered Daniel and said, "Truly your God is the God of gods, the Lord of kings, and the reveler of secrets, since you could reveal this secret."

5.  What stands out to you the most about today's lesson? Does anyone have an example of a dream they had before becoming a believer?

6.  Does anyone want to share a dream to interpret?

7.  **Objective** - students will understand why unbelievers have divine dreams.

8.  **Closing**

    a.  Any questions?

    b.  Homework: Read the other examples of dreams given to unbelievers.

        i.   Abimelech (Genesis 20:3-7). God warned him that he was about to sin.

        ii.  Pharoah (Genesis 41). God wanted to prepare Egypt (the world) for a coming crisis and elevate Joseph.

        iii. Nebechadnezzar (Daniel 4). God wanted to humble Nebuchadnezzar and show His sovereignty over all kings and nations.

        iv.  Closing prayer.

# Notes

# VISIONS: WHEN ANGELS APPEAR

Items need:

Bibles Journals

1. **Welcome and Opening Prayer**

   a. Ask for someone to recap last week's lesson.

   b. Ask who did their homework and would like to discuss any revelations or insight.

2. **Question: Who Has Encountered an Angel Before? What Did You Do? How Did You Feel?**

   a. What is a vision? "Supernatural revelation or divine communication from God, often given while a person is awake. It's how God makes His will, plans, or messages known beyond ordinary sight or understanding."

   b. Visions are initiated by God, not by human imagination.

   c. Visions allows a person to see into the spiritual realm (angels, future events or God's glory). Isaiah 6:1 - I saw the Lord sitting upon a throne, high and lifted up.

   d. Read Luke 1:11-22 (Zacharias' Visitation)

   e. What do you notice about this passage of scripture?

   f. This vision did not have to be interpreted because the angel spoke.

   g. Scriptures about angels in the Bible:

i. Angels are God's messengers (Genesis 16:7-12, Genesis 18:1-15 and other scriptures mentioned above).

ii. Angels act as protectors and warriors (Psalm 91, Exodus 23:20-23).

iii. Angels act as worshippers and servants of God (Isaiah 6:1-3, Hebrews 1:6).

iv. There are more but we will continue next week.

3. **Objective** - students will learn the purposes of angels.

4. **Activation**

   a. Spend quiet time with soaking worship music. Pray in the spirit. Journal what you sense (hear, see, smell, feel, etc).

   b. Hebrews 5:14 (KJV) - But strong meat belongeth to them that are of full age, even those who by reason of use have their senses exercised to discern both good and evil.

   c. Ask the students to share if they would like to.

5. **Closing**

   a. Homework - study the scriptures mentioned today.

   b. Prayer

# Notes

# VISIONS: WHEN ANGELS APPEAR PART II

Items needed:

Bible Journals

1. **Welcome and Opening Prayer**

   a.  Ask the students for a recap of last week's lesson.

   b.  Ask who did their homework. Discuss any questions or revelations.

2. **Teacher - Share Your Angelic Encounters. (Last Week The Students Were Asked to Share). Ask The Students What Role Did The Angel Appear in During The Encounter (Messenger, Protector, Guide, Or Worshipper).**

   a.  Read Luke 1:11-22 again.

   b.  Ask if anything new stands out about this passage.

   c.  Reiterate that this vision didn't have to be interpreted because the angel spoke.

   d.  Recap what we learned about angels last week. (Angels are God's messengers, protector, guide or worshipper. This week we will learn three more roles of angels.

   e.  Angels bring revelation and guidance (Acts 8:26, Daniel 8&9).

   f.  Angels as agents of judgment. Angels also carry out God's justice and judgment.

i. Genesis 19:1-29. The angels destroyed Sodom and Gomorrah but rescued Lot.

ii. II Kings 19:35. The angel of the Lord strikes down 185,000 Assyrian soldiers.

iii. Revelation 8-9, 15-16. Angels sound trumpets and pour out bowls of judgement in the end times.

g. Angels in ministry to believers.

i. Hebrews 1:14 - Are they not all ministering spirits sent forth to minister for those who will inherit salvation? "Kingdom Dynamics: ministering spirits, angels. A careful study will reveal that the NT activity of angels usually revolves around the ministry of Jesus and the establishment of His church on earth. They are ministering spirits or heavenly assistants who are continually active today in building the body of Christ - advancing the ministry of Jesus and the building of His church, (page 1731)."

h. Descriptions and Nature of Angels

i. Psalm 103:20 - Bless the Lord, you His angels, who excel in strength, who do His word, heeding the voice of His word.

ii. Ezekiel 1:4-14 - cherubim described with wings and radiant forms.

iii. Daniel 10:5-6 (read it).

iv. Luke 24:4 (angels appeared in dazzling clothes at Jesus' resurrection).

v. Hebrews 13:2 - Do not forget to entertain strangers, for by doing some have entertained angels.

vi. Ask the students if they have any questions.

3. **Objective** - students will learn the purposes of angels and activate their spiritual senses.

4. **Activation**

    a.  Prophetic Journaling. Play soaking worship music. Pray in the spirit and ask the student to journal what they sense (see, smell, hear, feel etc).

    b.  Ask for volunteers to share.

    c.  Ask if anyone has any questions.

5. **Close In Prayer. No Homework.**

# Notes

# MARY'S VISITATION

Items need:

Bibles Journals

1. **Welcome And Opening Prayer**

a. Ask for a recap of last week.

2. **Introduction To Mary's Visitation**

    a. Ask: Who knows who Mary is? Why is she important?

    b. Read: Luke 1:26-38

    c. Ask: Who is Gabriel? (The archangel sent to announce the will of God to man).

    d. What do you notice about this visitation?

    e. What do you notice about this visitation compared to Zacharias' visitation (Luke 1:11-22)?

        i. Both Mary and Luke asked a question after Gabriel spoke but only Zacharias was muted.

        ii. They both were troubled.

3. **Activation: Notice Mary's response to Gabriel. Let it be to me according to your word (Luke 1:38).** This should be our heart posture when we receive a prophetic word from a true messenger of God (no I am not calling prophets, angels).

a. Assign each student a partner. Everyone will pray in the spirit for a few minutes and ask the Holy Spirit to give them a prophetic word/vision for their partner. Write it down in each other's journals so they will always have it. Also, release the words aloud to each other and pray over the word.

b. If you're going through this curriculum alone, ask Holy Spirit to bring to your remembrance a prophecy/vision that you may have doubted because it hasn't come to pass yet and begin to war (pray) for that prophecy.

4. **Objective** - students will learn how to prophesy to each other and war for prophesy.

5. **Closing**

a. Any questions?

b. No homework.

# Notes

# MARY & ELIZABETH

Items Needed:

Bibles Journals

1. **Welcome And Opening Prayer**

   a. Ask a student to recap last week's lesson.

2. **Introduction: Sing Unto the Lord.**

   a. Text Luke 1: 39-56

   b. Ask: What do you notice about this text?

3. **Objective** - students will learn to praise God for what He's doing and what He will do.

4. **Activation**

   a. Students will spend time listening to soaking worship music and praying in the spirit.

   b. Students will ask the Holy Spirit to give them a song/poem about what God is doing or what He will do.

   c. Ask for volunteers to share their song/poem with the class.

5. **Closing**

   a. Homework: ask God if you have a purpose partner and who is it?

# Notes

# THE SHEPHERDS' VISION

Items needed:

Bibles

Journals

1.  **Welcome and Opening Prayer**

    a.  Ask a volunteer to recap last week's lesson.

    b.  Ask a volunteer if they completed their homework.

2.  **Introduction: The Shepherds' Vision**

    a.  Luke 2:1-20.

    b.  Define glory = splendor, radiance, majesty.

    c.  What stands out to you in this passage of scripture?

    d.  Let's think back to lessons 27 and 28 where we learned about the role of angels. What role were they performing in this passage of scripture? (messenger, worshiper, protector, minister, bringing revelation, agents of judgment or guides).

    e.  Vs. 12 - and this will be a sign to you. Ask. Why do you believe signs are important? Sign = a miraculous event, symbol or object given by God to confirm His word, reveal His will or confirm His messenger.

    f.  Has anyone ever asked God for a sign? Let's talk about it. Teacher note: If the students don't have one, the teacher can use their example or use three examples:

    i.   Gideon - Judges 6:36-40.

    ii.   Hezekiah - II Kings 20:8-11

    iii.   Ahaz - Isaiah 7:10-14.

  g.  Ask if anyone has any questions.

3. **Objective** - students will learn that God can use signs to confirm His word.

4. **Activation** - play soaking worship music and invite children to pray and ask the Lord to give them a sign for a word/vision that is to come to pass and to journal it. When everyone is done, invite the class to have a praise session. Luke 2:20 - Then the shepherds returned, glorifying and praising God for all the things that they had heard and seen, as it was told to them.

5. **Closing:** ask if anyone has any questions. No homework. End in prayer.

# Notes

# SIMEON'S REVELATION

Items needed:

Bibles Journals

1. **Welcome and Opening Prayer**

   a. Ask a volunteer to recap last week's lesson.

2. **Introduction: Simeon's Revelation Luke 2:22-35**

   a. Read or ask a volunteer to read Luke 2: 22-35.

   b. Ask your students what stands out to them the most? What do they have questions about?

   c. Highlight vs 25 & 26

      i. …the Holy Spirit was upon Him and it was revealed to him by the Holy Spirit that he would not see death before he had seen the Lord's Christ.

      ii. What does it mean for the Holy Spirit to be "upon you."

3. God's Spirit has come to rest on you with power, purpose, divine enablement, equipping you for service and supernatural work according to God's will.

4. Acts 1:8 - But you shall receive power when the Holy Spirit has come upon you and you shall be my witnesses…

5. Ask your students what Simeon did after the Holy Spirit came upon him. Give them time to think. He prophesied to Mary and Joseph.

d.  What happens when the Spirit comes upon you?

   i.  Boldness - Acts:31.

   ii.  Wisdom and revelation beyond your natural understanding - Isaiah 11:2.

   iii.  Spiritual gifts operate through you - I Corinthians 12:7-11

   iv.  A sense of divine presence and direction in life, work or ministry - Luke 3:22.

   v.  To bring glory to Jesus - John 16:14.

   vi.  You become empowered to do what you can't do on your own.

   vii.  Scripture references: Judges 14:16 and Luke 4:18.

   viii. Important note: The Holy Spirit is within us which means His indwelling presence - the Spirit living inside every believer after salvation (John 14:7 and Romans 8:9). When the Holy Spirit comes upon you, it is referring to an outpouring or empowerment - a special anointing for action, boldness, or divine assignment.

6.  **Objective** - students will learn what it means when the Spirit of the Lord comes upon us.

7.  **Activation -** Pray in the spirit for several minutes. Ask the Holy Spirit to come upon you and give you a prophetic word for yourself. Journal it. Ask volunteers to share with the group. For younger students: Ask the Holy Spirit to show them Jesus. Have them draw a picture.

8.  **Closing:** ask your students if they have any questions. Homework: Study the scriptures mentioned today about the Holy Spirit coming upon you. Close in prayer.

# Notes

# JOHN THE BAPTIST AND JESUS

Items Needed:

Bibles Journals

Song: Rest On Us - Maverick City

1. **Welcome and Opening Prayer.**

   a. Ask for a volunteer to recap last week's lesson.

   b. Ask for a volunteer who did their homework to share.

2. **Introduction: John The Baptist and Jesus**

   a. Who remembers who John is to Jesus?

   b. Read Luke 3: 15-22

   c. Read Matthew 3: 11-17 (I personally like Matthew's account better than Luke's because it is more detailed).

   d. What do you all notice about this passage of scripture?

   e. Last week we learned about the Spirit coming upon us. In this passage the Spirit came upon Jesus. Why do you think Jesus needed the Holy Spirit?

   f. Matthew 3:11b - He will baptize you with the Holy Spirit and fire.

      i. We need to accept Jesus to receive the Holy Spirit. Jesus is the baptizer with the Holy Spirit.

ii. Jesus saves us and then wants to ongoingly fill us, pouring the Holy Spirit upon us so we can demonstrate the living power of Jesus wherever we go.

3. **Objective** - students will learn that Jesus needed the Holy Spirit to fulfill His mission and we do too. We also need Jesus to receive the Holy Spirit.

4. **Activations**

    a. Invite any new students to accept Jesus Christ as their Lord and Savior.

    b. Pray together as a group in the spirit. Ask the Lord for a fresh infilling of His Spirit. Surrender fully to Holy Spirit

5. **Close In Prayer. No Homework.**

# Notes

# SAUL/PAUL'S VISION OF CHRIST

Items Needed:

Bibles Journals

1. **Welcome and Opening Prayer**

   a. Ask for a volunteer to recap last week's lesson.

   b. Ask if anyone has any questions.

2. **Introduction: Saul/Paul's Vision of Christ**

   a. Read Acts 9: 1-22.

   b. What do we notice about his passage of scripture?

   c. Paul's dramatic conversion is proof of the validity of Christianity.

   d. Paul had a vision, he was baptized, filled with the Holy and then he went to preach the gospel.

   e. Preach = publicly proclaim the gospel - the good news of Jesus Christ and encourage repentance and forgiveness of sins.

   f. I call what Paul experienced "Divine Strategy," it is the blueprint. Once you have a conversion, it is your responsibility to share the gospel. Paul was a walking, talking, living testimony that Jesus is the Son of God.

   g. Acts 22:1-21 and Acts 26:12-18 (Apostle Paul shares his testimony).

3. **Objective** - students will learn how to share their testimony/story to draw others to Jesus.

4. **Application:** Ask students to share their testimony (two-three minutes) about how they came to Christ so that they will be comfortable with sharing it with others for the glory of God.

5. **Closing:** ask if they have any questions. Homework: Ask God to highlight someone for you to share your testimony with and share it. Close in prayer

# Notes

# PAUL'S VISIONS

Items Needed:

Bibles Journals

Map or Globe

1. **Welcome And Opening Prayer**

   a.  Ask for someone to recap last week's lesson.

   b.  Ask for a volunteer who has done the homework to share.

2. **Introduction: After His Conversion, Apostle Paul Continued to Have Visions.**

   a.  Read Acts 16:9-15. He was on a mission to spread the gospel.

   b.  What do you notice from this passage of scripture?

   c.  Paul was being sent to a specific city but on the way he was still being a witness and sharing the gospel.

   d.  Any questions.

3. **Objective** - students will pray about what city/nation God wants them to pray for to receive the gospel.

4. **Activation** - ask the students to pray and ask the Holy Spirit to reveal to them what city/nation God wants them to pray for. Journal it and pray for them. Ask the Lord if there is anything else He wants to do in that city/nation. Ask for volunteers to share with the group.

5. **Homework** - pray for that city/nation all week and watch for good news, changes or reports.

6. **Close In Prayer.**

# Notes

# ALL THINGS WORK TOGETHER FOR GOOD

Items needed:

Bible Journals

1. **Welcoming and Opening Prayer**

   a. Ask for a volunteer to recap last week's lesson.

   b. Ask for a volunteer that did their homework to share.

2. **Introduction: Paul and Silas Imprisoned**

   a. Read Acts 16:16-34

   b. What do you notice about this passage of scripture?

   c. When you serve the Lord, people will try to mock you, but they are mocking God.

   d. Paul and Silas rejoiced in the midst of their circumstances and someone's whole household was saved. Romans 8:28

   e. Acts 18:9-10. The Lord's promise to Paul is His promise to all of us.

   f. Ask: Has any situation happened in your life that you thought was "bad" but it brought glory to God?

3. **Objective** - students are encouraged to be living witnesses for God and not to fear people and that all things work together for good.

4. **Activation** - Pair students up. Ask them to pray for each other and ask the Holy Spirit to give them a word to encourage their partner. Some students

may even receive songs to sing or scriptures. Release the word and pray for each other. Make sure students journal their words.

5. **Homework** - study the book of Acts.

6. **Closing Prayer**

# Notes

# PROPHET IN THE NEW TESTAMENT: AGABUS

Items needed:

Bibles Journals

1.  **Welcoming And Opening Prayer**

    a.  Ask for a volunteer to recap last week's lesson.

    b.  Ask for a volunteer any insight/thoughts from reading the Book of Acts.

2.  **Introduction - Agabus**

    a.  Who knows who Agabus is? We've talked mostly about visions and dreams in the New Testament. Now we will learn of a New Testament Prophet, Agabus. )This is extremely important for people that argue prophets are only in the Old Testament.

    b.  Acts 11: 27-30.

    c.  What do we notice about this passage of scripture?

        i.   The church took action to meet the need of the challenging situation.

    d.  Agabus stood in the office of a prophet. There is the office of a prophet which is different from the gift of prophecy.

    e.  The office of the prophet = a Christ appointed ministry of a person. Their role includes guidance, correction, direction and foundational ministry. Old Testament examples are Samuel, Elijah, Elisha, Jeremiah, Isaiah.

f.  The gift of prophecy = the Holy Spirit distributes the gift through a person to edify (build up), exhort (encourage) and comfort the church. Every believer has access. (I Corinthians 14:3).

g.  Acts 21:8-14 - Apostle Paul was warned by Agabus.

h.  Acts 21:30-32 - Agabus' prophecy was fulfilled.

    i.  If Paul was warned why do you think he still went?

    ii.  Has the Lord sent you any divine warnings? How did it turn out?

3.  **Objective** - students will learn the difference between the gift of prophecy and the office of a prophet.

4.  **Activation** - Play soaking worship music. Worship the Lord for His goodness and mercy. Thank him for protection and safety (even in famine). Have sweet fellowship with God.

5.  **Close In Prayer. No Homework.**

# Notes

**Celebrate! You made it through 37 lessons!** Have a celebration with your students. Ask them which lessons were their favorite. Ask them how they have grown and if there is anything they would like to share.

My prayer is that each and every person that this curriculum touches will be transformed and go out and change the world for Jesus and that revival will be birthed in each individual. I pray that everyone receives a hunger for Christ and the Word of God. Let your children know how important they are to Jesus. Mark 10:14 16 NKJV - Jesus says, "Let the little children come to Me, and do not forbid them; for of such is the kingdom of God. Assuredly I say to you, whoever does not receive the kingdom of God as a little child will by no means enter it." And He took them up in His arms, laid His hands on them, and blessed them.

Never stop growing in the Lord. Be the salt and light of the Lord.

*All scriptures used are from the New Spirit Filled Life Bible NKJV. Nelson 2552. Please send questions, testimonies and inquiries to book37.montiajanuary@gmail.com